Real Estate Investing

A Beginner's Guide to Rental Income and Long-Term Wealth

Julian Ashford

ISBN:9781807650452

Published by TPSA Publishing

Catalog

INTRODUCTION

Real estate has a reputation for being "the safe way to get wealthy." You buy a property, collect rent, watch the value rise, and—somewhere down the line—financial stress starts to loosen its grip. In reality, that promise is only half the story. Real estate can absolutely create rental income and long-term wealth, but it does it through decisions—sometimes small, sometimes expensive—that stack up over time. The difference between a life-changing asset and a slow-moving financial headache usually isn't luck. It's clarity, structure, and the ability to evaluate opportunities without getting swept up by hype.

That's what this book is for. Real Estate Investing: A Beginner's Guide to Rental Income and Long-Term Wealth is designed to be your practical entry point into the real estate world—especially the side of real estate that actually builds wealth: buying with purpose, understanding risk, setting a strategy, and managing your investment like a business.

This book moves in a logical sequence—starting with the foundation and gradually building toward execution and optimization. You'll begin by grounding yourself in what real estate investing actually means: using tangible, immovable property (land, buildings, apartments) to generate returns—most commonly through rent, appreciation, or both. From there, you'll learn why people invest in real estate, what makes it attractive compared to other investments, and what limitations you need to respect.

This book won't pretend that real estate is effortless, and it won't promise you instant wealth. What it can do is more valuable: it can give you a clear foundation—so you can make informed decisions, avoid costly beginner mistakes, and build a strategy that fits your goals, your budget, and your risk tolerance.

If you commit to learning and applying what's here, real estate can become more than an idea. It can become a tool—one that generates income, builds equity, and gradually moves you toward financial stability and long-term wealth.

Let's begin!

CHAPTER ONE: INTRODUCTION TO REAL ESTATE INVESTMENT

Welcome to the first chapter of the book. From the name you already got the idea about the book. Yes, this is the book about the investment process in the real estate market. Well, the concept might be common that several businessmen around your area or several familiar people might be involved with this. From there, you might hear about the matter of the real estate business. But you don't have proper knowledge of the thing, which brings you to read this book. Here, in this book, I will show you the way of the real estate investment. I think this book will give you the basic idea about the thing. If well practical knowledge is the best thing that you would want to learn. With this book, I won't be able to show the whole picture that you would get on a practical field. Rather I will give you the preliminary entry on the real estate market.

Real estate

You know the meaning of real estate. The real here means a practical or physical thing whereas estate means property, land, grounds, park, parkland, and several others which you know. Just combine the two words you will get the meaning of the thing. So the real estate is dealing with the practical property or asset that is tangible. The property which is not tangible does not come under this term. Say your house, building, land which are tangible assets for you can be dealt with real estate. Other properties like the trademark of your business, goodwill, license, and different intellectual properties do not come under this term.

[NB: Tangible assets are those which can be physically located, touched or seen such as land, buildings, products, machinery, equipment, and so on. On the other hand, intangible assets are those which cannot be touched or seen rather these assets can be recognized in the virtual form such as goodwill, brand, trademark and several other.]

Investment

Well, investment is a simple and common term that almost everyone understands. Investment refers to the employment of capital or fund and making a profit from the employment of funds or capital. Suppose you have €1000 available cash in your hand. But you don't want to spend and finish the amount, rather you want to employ the amount and make a profit so that you can make your spending from your profit and the principal €1000 remain the same or increase. So you bought an automobile and lend it to a person who will use it and give you €50 per month. The ownership with the lending does not change you are still the owner, the person is just using your asset for a certain payment. In the end, you will have €50 every month which you can use and you still have your major investment in that automobile which you can get back by selling in the market. Of course, there is a depreciation of the automobile which will not let you get back the whole amount. Well, that is the risk of investment. The investment is a huge chapter to discuss. Here you can conclude with this basic idea about investment.

Real Estate Investment

Well, we have seen the meaning of every individual term, now it is time to conclude all of them in a single raw. So the real estate investment means using the property that is physical or tangible for investment purposes and makes a profit for the future. Moreover, the term means to invest in the properties that are tangible like the lands, buildings mostly immovable properties. If you just think that all the tangible asset comes under real estate investment, then it will confuse you with this definition. The real estate investment is investing in the assets or properties that are tangible and immovable and using them to generate a certain return and cover the investment to gain more. The basic asset that is being worked with is the investment in the land, building, and properties. The most common idea that can give you is the use of these properties for rental disbursement and get the return. For the rental use, you need to own the property and lend other for use.

Let's take you to an example which might give you a clear idea about the term. Mr. Roberto is a retired police officer. He had an amount of savings which he had collected over his professional life. Now the savings remain idle. So he wants to use them and make a profit from the amount. He invested some portion of the amount in the stock market, some portion in his friend's business some in government bond and still he has €300000 to invest. So with this amount Mr. Roberto buys an apartment in Milan city. Mr. Roberto wants to rent the apartment to other people to live in that apartment for €1000 per month. So this will give a monthly income of €1000 from the investment. This is a basic scenario of real estate investment. Hope this gave you the basic idea of the matter.

Now you might think that it's easier than you thought before. Well, the concept will get more complex when you will get into the investment market. The more you go deep, the more you will understand the concept and be efficient about the investment. The investment in real estate is more sometimes get riskier than it looks. So you need to be very sincere while deciding about your investment. I am here presenting this book to you as the guide to the investment pros and cons.

Why Invest In Real Estate?

The basic reason for your investment is getting profit. Perhaps, there are several opportunities for you to invest and make a profit from them. So, for investing in real estate, there should be some solid reason for choosing the real estate investment over other investments.

Think that Mr. Roberto is getting sufficient profit from his bond market and share market investment. Now here two different scenarios can be established with imagination to make a clear view of the matter. First is that he wants to get back the amount of investment in the apartment by selling the apartment. With the amount, he wants to invest them in the stock market since the stock market is giving him more return than the real estate investment. On the second scenario, he keeps the amount invested and raise more capital to invest in another investment since he is getting a regular income compared to the stock market as well as the amount he invested is secured with the apartment. Both of the scenarios can come to existence. It depends on the nature of investment and the decision of the investor.

An investor has several choices for investment and making a profit from an investment. Now, as an investor, you will invest in real estate business if you get enough return from your investment and more security than other investments. Now you might be thinking about why you should invest in real estate? Well, there are a couple of advantages that the investment in real estate will give you which might not be present or partially present in other investments. So, here I am showing you some of the benefits that you can get from your investment in the real estate: **Fixed or predictable return:** The return in real estate investment is predictable where you can evaluate how much it worth with the time-lapse. From the example of Mr. Roberto, it can be seen that he is receiving €1000 every month from his apartment rent. Here one thing that is to be noted is that real estate mostly uses of the rental property that the investor can lend others for use and get a periodic return from the rent.

Inflation-adjusted: The return or the principal investment that you invested in the real estate or property is adjusted with the inflation of your economy. The rents that you get from your property will increase depending on the increase in the inflation rate. Now think that the rate of the inflation in your economy is rising up so the value of the asset in your economy will also rise. Now you have invested in some property which will also rise accordingly following the rise of the price in the economy.

Leveraging: An important advantage that you can get from the investment is the benefit of leverage. Suppose Mr. Roberto Wants to buy another apartment that he can lend with €1200, but he does not have enough resources or funds with him. So he can borrow some portion of the required funds to buy another apartment. He can borrow the fund from a bank, or another source where he can pay the interest amount with the rent he receives from the rent of the apartment. These allow him to own a new apartment and pay off the loan amount from the rent. The benefit of this investment is owning an apartment.

Raise in Capital Value: Your main investment in the property gets you a regular income and additionally, the property value that you bought will increase with the lapse of time. You can evaluate the increase in present terms. Look around you, the value of the land and buildings are getting increased day by day. Your property will also increase with time.

Lower risk with the principal investment: While you invest in real property the investment does not go in vain. If you invest in the stock market, your investment might be at risk of facing loss and reduction in your funds. There is also a chance that most of your funds might vanish with the wrong investment. Here in real property the risk very little about the principal amount. If you invest in property your principal amount is secured with the immovable property. Remember the value of the immovable property does not vanish. Sometime it might get lower but that would not cost the principal amount of loss. Suppose if you have stock of a company that is not performing well in the market and incurring a loss, holding that share will cost you lose amount. Whereas the price of the stock will also decrease in value. On the contrary, if you own a land valuing €200000 it will not decrease in value over time. You can use it for lending others and get rent from it and the actual value or the principal amount will remain secured.

Limitations for investing in real estate

Everything has its positive and negative sides as well. In this chapter, you saw the advantages that you can get from your investment in real estate investing. Well, there are also some limitations or which you can say drawbacks also. While you invest in real estate, you might feel these lacking in the sector.

Lengthy liquidation: Think that you have a property that you are using as a real estate investment. Now you want to get some cashback in your hand. With the stocks and bonds in your hand, you can sell them easily at the market and liquidate your capital. But in the case of the real estate properties, you can also collect cash by selling them, but it is not so easy to find such customers instantly to sell a property like land or building within few moments. Besides, there would be so many formalities like the documentation for selling a property and several other causes will occur while liquidating your properties.

Fluctuation in value: The value of the real estate property can be variable depending on the price fluctuation of the market. The rental value, as well as the property value in the market, fluctuates over time. Generally, it does not occur with the lands or buildings but sometimes it takes place depending on the situation or location of the property. Imagine you have landed in a rural area. The government is planning to build up a new community in that area where you have land. With the government project in that area, your land value will increase. Now think conversely that instead of a new community, the government is trying to build a mining factory. This time your land value will decrease since most people will avoid buying land beside the mining factory because of the noise and pollution.

Maintenance of property: The property in real estate needs to be maintained for which you need to incur the cost. Maintaining the property will cost you higher as well as complexity with the tenants that you give rent to. Let's take you back to the example of Mr. Roberto who lends his apartment to tenants for rent. Now the apartment should be made ready before the tenant starts to use it. So Mr. Roberto has to furnish the apartment, clean it and make a repair where needed. Moreover, the maintenance of the apartment would cost Mr. Roberto some time as well as some money.

Complexity: In the case of the investment you have already noticed that there are some complexities. The handling of the property issues is to be done with so much lengthy and complex formalities which can be proved to be a burden for you. If you are really willing to invest in real estate property, you need to go through these complexities.

Transaction cost: the cost of transaction in real estate property is relay higher than other transactions.'

Types of Real Estate Investment

This is an introductory chapter for real estate investment. So for the clarification of the topic you need to know about the types of real estate investment. Basically, real estate works with practical and physical assets. Here the investment in the asset can be the same type. So the classification of these investments has been made depending on the use of the property. Depending on the use, properties can be divided into three parts,

1. Commercial Use: The investment in real estate property is basically made for commercial use. Now if you look on the motive, the first thing that might come to you is the use of the land or buildings for commercial use like office, a business organization that gives more return than general. The office building, lending for a storehouse, shops, shopping mall, etc. come under this term.
2. Industrial Use: Like the commercial use, you can also lend your property for industrial use. Like lending your land or building for factory or manufacturing business.
3. Residential Use: Residential use are mostly for the house, apartments, accommodational space. From the example of Mr.

Roberto, the apartment he bought for lending others for use is a type of residential property.

So, the types of investment depending on the purpose of use has been clarified. Now there are other two types of investing categories in real estate which you need to understand. Understanding these will help you to make the decision about your investing type. That vast type includes active investment and passive investment.

Active Real Estate Investment Like the name suggest. The active real estate investment refers to investing in real estate with the involvement of the investor. Elaborating the term we get that, the investor, while handling the properties with direct involvement i.e. direct buying and selling or lending of his properties, it comes under this term. I would like to give an example of this term. Such that Mr. Roberto who wants to buy an apartment. Goes to the owner and buys the property. After buying the property Mr. Roberto needs to modify the apartment as per requirement which is to be done by his involvement. Afterward, Mr. Roberto needs to find out the customer by himself whom he is going to lend the property. Moreover, all the activities from the starting to the end, the activities are done with the direct involvement of the investor in this type of investment.

Passive Real Estate Investment From the previous example, you might get an idea about passive investment. Well, you are right, this is just opposite to the active style of investment. Some of the investors just want to maximize their return on capital. They don't want to be part of any complexity. So they might choose this type of investing style. Here the investors are required to choose the agents who are actively working with the real estate operations. Those agents will invest and manage your funds and properties according to your instructions. Now look again on the scenario of Mr. Roberto, where being an old person, Mr. Roberto does not want to involve in these complex activities of real estate. So he calls upon an agent who works with the real estate investment. Now Mr. Roberto instructs the agent to purchase an apartment of choice for Mr. Roberto and allow the apartment for rental use. Now the agent will do the tasks that Mr. Roberto would do with the active involvement in the investment like maintaining the properties, repairing, finding clients and users, and other formalities. Of course, the agent will charge a commission. But here Mr. Roberto just having a benefit from the investment on the properties with the lower complexity of being involved in these activities.

Learning Outcome from This Chapter

Well, after reading and understanding this chapter you would be able to learn the following thing: You will have a primary idea of the investment in real estate property.

You will be able to conclude about the real estate property.

You will also be able to invest in rental property.

You can evaluate the type of investment.

You will be able to decide which type of investor you want to be.

CHAPTER TWO: BASIC TERMINOLOGY FOR NEW INVESTORS

Now, you have a basic idea about the investment. So you are now able to invest in real estate property. But this is not all, there are a lot of factors which you need to learn about real estate investment. This book will show you the aspects that businessman in real estate follows. Following these, you will know the procedures that the corporate investors follow. Theoretical knowledge cannot reveal all the things clearly to you. But here I will try to show those aspects with an example which will be helpful for you to understand the matter. Like the previous chapter, this chapter has been furnished with the terminology which you need to know for further knowledge and entrance in the real estate investment phase. So let's start with the terminologies.

Rental Properties

The first in this list comes the turn of rental properties that you already know about. The rental properties are those which can be lent for use to tenants and the owner of the property gets a regular payment as rent. Here the term tenants can be mentioned as the user who will take the property and use it for the interest of the tenant. Moreover, the tenant will occupy the property and use it as the owner might do and pay the rent to the owner. The apartment that Mr. Roberto bought and give rent to a tenant is a type of rental property for Mr. Roberto since he gets a monthly payment from his apartment. There are several forms of rental properties such as a house for rent, apartments for rent, office building for rent, storage rent and so on.

REITs

This is a vast term that you should learn about while entering into real estate investment. The look at the word, it is formed with four latter which definitely stands for another word. With the combination of those words, it creates another meaning. Let's break the thing, R stands for Real, E stands for Estate, I stands for Investment, and T stands for Trust. So the meaning of the word comes with the trust in the investment in the real estate property which suggests that it a trusted organization or institution which is involved in the real estate investment. The REIT is an organization that is in control of the investments in real estate properties such as buying, monitoring, executing, finding clients, collecting rents and so on. The REITs act as an agent for the investors. Not all investors are able to invest in large property alone. To buy a property like a house, land, or apartment it takes large amounts, which seems tough for some investors who can give their investment fund to REIT. REIT collects funds from several investors and invest in real estate properties for the investors and maintains the procedures of investment. It acts as mutual funds that distribute the profit after a certain period but it is not mutual fund. The main motive of this organization is to allow all the investors to have the opportunity to invest in real estate properties. The organization also reduces the complexity of the tasks related to real estate properties.

Consider a scenario of some other investors who are not able to buy an apartment like Mr. Roberto. There are several investors who have little savings, those investors can form a large amount of fund by rendering their saving to the REIT organization and where the organization will use the funds for the investment in real estate. Like mutual funds, REIT also uses the return to distribute to the investors depending on their portion of the investment. Any investment company can act as REIT. Here are certain characteristics of the organization which should be present on an organization for being REIT.

∞ The first and foremost characteristics are that the company needs to invest at least 75% of the funds in rental properties from where it can collect rent as a regular profit and distribute to the investors.

∞ Also, it should have its collection of profit from the rental source. The portion of the profit that should be collected from the rental property is also 75%.

∞ Here comes the main characteristic which bears the identity of the trust. The organization must distribute 90% of the profit to the investors.

There are different types of REITs depending on the types of investment. Such as *Equity REITs:* Invests in the properties that are rental equity producing a regular income.

Mortgage REITs: Provides the opportunity to invest in the properties with the back up by mortgaging the properties.

Private REITs: The organization handles only investment in private sectors and private properties.

Hybrid REITs: Own properties as well as make mortgages for the backup funding.

Inflation Hedging

To evaluate this term you need to know the terms individually. Do you know what inflation is? Inflation is the state of the economy in which the currency of the economy loses its value. Or the purchasing power of the currency decreases. Of course in this scenario, the level of the price of the commodity rises. On the other hand, hedging is an investment appraisal procedure that takes initiatives against the adverse price or rate movement. In short, it will defend the fluctuation of interest rate and inflation rate in the economy.

So the term, in the real estate works with the rate of inflation. The inflation hedging is one kind of protectionism in the investment of real estate properties. Suppose you invest in real estate such land which you have bought with €200000. With the inflation in funds that you get from selling the property might not be equal to the value of that fund in the present term. So you can opt for an inflation hedging which will protect you from such risk with the premium payment while inflation rises.

Real estate is a great sector that can play a vital role in your hedging of the properties from the risk of an increase in the inflation rate. The investors in this sector generally invest in such types of properties which gives a regular and updated return. Mostly the rental properties are the most effective investment for hedging the funds against an increase in the inflation rate. Since the rental properties will give you the return monthly so the rate of the rent or price can be adjusted depending on the inflation rate of the economy.

Real Estate Partnership

Basically, partnership is the way of combination of two or more people where they act together to achieve a certain goal. In case of business you might have the basic idea about partnership. In the real estate sector, partnership means the person with whom you can invest in a combination. Here the term comes to RELP which stands for real estate limited partnership. The partnership in real estate means to collect funds of different people who are in the partnership. Use the fund to purchase the required properties and maintain them to generate profit from the properties. In most of the scenarios, the partnership goal is to make a diversified return from a portfolio investment.

[NB: Portfolio is the term that allows to invest in different asset rather than investing in single asset to minimize the risk of the fund loss. Since there are some possibilities that the investment will go in vain, so the financial experts suggest the investment in diversified asset so that the return is assured from any of the asset. The general belief in portfolio making is that, if one asset generate loss another will fill the loss with more profit.]

The partnership in real estate is not like other general partnership. The partners might act like other types of partnership but here the duties and responsibilities in real estate partnership is different from other types of partnership. In real estate the partners form a group which is for collection of funds from the member of the group of partners. In previous term REIT, I have shown you the way of investors where several investors can invest this can be compared to that scenario. The difference is that in case of REITs the organization play the role for maintaining the investment and other procedures but in RELPs the partners are devoted to the team of partners for the achievement of their targeted return from their investment.

An example can be given. Imagine you have a limited fund you want invest in real estate properties. But due to limitation of capital or fund, you cannot invest in real estate properties. So you are looking for another investors from your community. You have found five persons who are willing to invest with you. So collecting the funds from all the partners, you gathered a large amount which you can invest in land or apartments and use them for rent.

Flip side

Flip side means to take an opposite position. Flip side is the most devastating side of the real estate investment. It refers to the trading that takes place between the investors of the real estate sector. Like stock market the real estate market also works as trading among the investors. The most attracting point in this trading is that the amount of trading is greater in real estate that happens within a very few time. Till now I have discussed the basic form of real estate investment. Now with this term I will show you how the real estate business is running in current world. The tactics that is being used by the investors are like the investors in the money market with short term investment. Previously I explained about the real estate market that it is much liquid market where the real estate investors do not invest money for long term. Many of the real estate investors now invest for a short term trading and seeking profit from them.

For example let's say Mr. Roberto have bought an apartment. Now there are so many complexity with the apartment like the repair of the apartment, finding out client and so on. Now Mr. Roberto considers quick return on the investment so he initiates sales of the apartment rather than maintaining the apartment which will get him back the investment amount also he can make some profit if he can sell them with higher price. With this he can avoid the complexity of handling and maintaining the apartment as well as getting back the invested amount sooner. Now Mr. Roberto realizes that the price of the apartment has increased which results in a capital gain from that investment. So he is likely to opt for more opportunity like that one.

Like Mr. Roberto, there are many investors who initiates and look forward to have the capital gain from buying a selling the real estate properties. This is the matter of flip side. This types of investors do not expenses extra funds for the maintenance of the properties since the investors would not keep the property. The rapid buying and selling of the properties and making profit from the exchange is the motive of this types of the investors.

Real Estate Mutual Funds

Like stock market investment the real estate also have the opportunity of mutual fund. The mutual fund is the investment process that allows different investors to accumulate funds and gather a larger amount for investment and distribute the profit among them. The most devastating advantage of the mutual fund is that it acts just like the stock market mutual funds which is easier for the investors to handle and interpret the investment procedures. From this definition you might be confuse about the real estate mutual funds with the REITs. The same activities with the same purpose so what is the use of the term. Well for understanding the term, you need to evaluate the difference between the REITs and the mutual fund. So here are some of the differences that can make you understand both of the terms.

∞ The mutual fund is the collection of funds by the investors whereas the REITs collects their funds via the distribution of securities that acts like the share or share like securities.

∞ The mutual funds invest in different assets, there are no limitation or specific guideline of the investment, the investors will decide the investment depending on their profit or investment desire. On the contrary, the investment in the REITs have to be made accordingly with the regulation which indicates ¾ part of the investment funds should be invested in the rental properties.

∞ The investment of the REITs are mostly made in the mortgages and real properties whereas the mutual funds sometimes invest in the REITs and other securities.

From the difference of the terms, you might be clear of the terms. The motive of mutual fund and REITs are almost similar which is allowing the investors to have the benefits of the large amount investment consisting the valued properties. Thus the mutual fund is easier for the investors to initiate with the investment process and employ their funds in the investment and make profits. Like he REITs the mutual fund also allows the investors to have the advantage of diversified investment.

Diversification

Well, this term might seem familiar with the financial term. If you have an understanding of financial terms, you might hear about this, but if you are not, then this short introduction about diversification is for you to understand the term. The term refers to the technique of selecting and investing which minimize the risk of the overall investment. The risk in the real estate might occur due to the fluctuations in price, negative cash flows, fraudulent activities by clients and tenants, structural risk, risk with location and so on which might be effective on the return of the properties.

Now you might ask why diversification? Well, the investment in the properties bears a certain risk. The risk can be varied depending on the asset types. Making a portfolio investment can reduce your risk of the investment. In this sense the diversification of your properties according to the risk and types of risk and making the portfolio will be most perfect reduction of your risk and optimization of your portfolio return.

[NB: Portfolio is investment procedures for minimizing the overall risk of investment by investing in different types of asset. The theme of the portfolio is that if one asset gets negative return, then another asset will cover the loss with positive return. It is assumed that investing in 2 asset will secure your fund more than investing in single asset.]

In some scenarios, the risk might not be less, while you are expecting a high return portfolio you might incur some risk on your overall portfolio. The formation of a portfolio works on the overall risk related to the investment. But the diversification works with an individual security risk. Now diversification of your property investment is for the motive of managing the risk of every property you are investing in. Now before making your investment decision you should consider diversifying your property and incur lower risk as much as possible.

Protectionism

Look at the meaning of the term, the protectionism is related to protecting or defending something. Here in this case, we are discussing the real estate investment terms. So here the protection against the risk of investment would come while we discuss the term. Protectionism is the policies that are followed by investors for the protection of their funds and trading of their properties. It is mainly related to the cross border transactions. In case of real estate properties, the protectionism is the protection policies for the properties and documentations since there might be chances for fraudulent activities. The protectionism create the opportunities for taking initiatives against the unfavorable movement in the trading of the real estate properties.

Leverage

Leverage refers to the investment process in which the funds for the investment might not be yours. So the where from the funds come. Borrow money from the sources that might be easier for you. The process includes borrowing most of the funds for investment and pay of the borrowed funds from the return from the investment. Let me clarify you with an example.

Let's assume Mr. Roberto who bought an apartment, does not have funds for buying another apartment for his trading. He has only partial amount as €100000 but he needs €300000 for buying the new apartment. Now he wishes to lend the rest of the amount €200000 from friends, or other financial source. From buying the property at €300000, he sells the apartment for €320000. After a quick trading of the apartment Mr. Roberto made a profit of €20000 within a month. So now he gives back the borrowed funds from friends and other sources with interests. So now with the utilization of the borrowed money he gets the profit from the investment. This procedures is the technique of the leverage.

So the basic concept of leverage is the utilizing borrowed funds and making positive return from the borrowed fund. The leverage in the real estate sector refers to your ability to use other's funds to get your expected return. So you will have to be very selective in investing the funds of other investors and make the right use of the funds. The portion of the funds that is borrowed compared to the funds that is yours is the leverage. In the real estate scenario, the funds are mostly used in the trading where the funds are returned within shorter terms. Although there are some risk, the investors like to initiate the risk for the return that generates from funds.

Learning Outcomes of This Chapter

After reading and understanding the terms in this chapter you will be able to learn The terms that are most common in the real estate investment scenario.

The learning terms might include the rental properties, REITs, inflation, hedging, flip side, mutual funds, diversification, protectionism, leverage.

With these terms, you also got the understanding of some other terminologies that came to light while discussing these terms.

CHAPTER THREE: INVESTMENT PROCEDURES IN REAL ESTATE

Guidance for the investment process

Well, now you have idea about the investment in the real estate properties. You got some basic knowledge about the properties that are traded in real estate. Now you think you will go and buy the properties of your choice! But wait there are certain things that you should consider before making the choice of your properties and make investment. This chapter is about the guidance of investment procedures that will take you to the investment procedure. By following these procedures, you will be able to select the best properties that is suitable for your funds and meets your requirements. So, here are some steps which you can apply while initiating your investment process.

Identifying the Funds Availability

Do you know, what is the first thing that is required for an investment? Fund or the capital is the first requirement for an investment. If you don't fund you won't be able to make an investment. So for the initiation of the investment process in real estate business you need to determine your available fund for investment. You might have lot of asset or funds or capital. But all are not for investment, some part of the fund might be preserved for other use. Like the business organization, personal balance also requires management and determination of the funds available for use in investment purpose. Do you remember the example of Mr. Roberto where I showed you about his financial condition? In that example I stated about the investment availability of Mr. Roberto. Mr. Roberto had enough fund, but he did not put all the fund in real estate investment. Rather he used some portion of the funds into real estate investment. Like Mr. Roberto you also need to evaluate the availability of your fund which portion you can employ in the investment of real estate property. After the realization of the funds, you will proceed to other steps.

Getting the information about the property you want to invest.

This is the most common process that you would do if I do not tell you either. But do you know how to collect these information or which information should you collect? Here the information will guide you to the proper way of collecting the related information about the properties. There is a proverb goes "look before you leap". Most probably, maximum number of people for making a decision thinks about the incident and consequence of the decision that he/she takes. Here in the real estate sector you will also have to think about your investment and consider some factors. For the consideration and a research about the properties, you can collect the following information: Price

The first information that all the investor collects is the price of the asset. Most probably you would also even if I would not suggest you here. The price or the trade cost is the main indicator about your investment. You should get the information from real source. Assume Mr. Roberto trying to buy an apartment so he heard from a person about the apartment price. But the person he asks does not know the actual price of the apartment, so the person gives a wrong information. Or in some scenario the person might motive to make a fraudulent act with Mr. Roberto. So these might be conflicting for Mr. Roberto. He should seek for the seller or the current owner of the apartment. So the source of the information about the price should be clear and authentic.

It is not enough to know the price of the asset only. You should also get the information about the price of the similar asset in the market. This will allow you to compare the asset with other asset and select the best option in the market. Imagine again about the scenario of Mr. Roberto where he got the opportunity to buy the apartment with €300000. And after that he realizes that he could get another apartment with €250000. So after the purchase he realizes if he would buy another apartment with €250000 that would be more profitable for him. This conflict would not take place if Mr. Roberto would have collected the information about price in the market.

Location

Location is another crucial fact for the real estate investment. It is the location that decides the demand for your property. With more demand of your property the rent or price for your property goes higher. Now imagine again that you got an offer to buy an apartment. You bought the apartment and did not even visit the location and did not even get any information about the location. And after making the purchase you can't find any client or tenant for your apartment. Now, after intervention on the matter you see that the location of the apartment is far away from the locality for which no one is getting interested to buy or rent that apartment.

Similarly there might be different scenario where your property might loss attraction of your client. Among the location problem the major are Problems with transportation Being far from locality or destination Being in rural area Beside mining factory or forestland.

Infrastructural problem Problem with basic facilities like, water, foods, markets and so on.

When these problems arise with your properties you might be in the risk that your property would lose the value that you expect. So you should always be aware of the location of your property.

Owner

You should get the information about the current owner of the property. With the owner of the property there might be chance to initiate fraudulent activities. Think that you are willing to buy a land in your locality. Now you got an offer from a person who is willing to sell a land to you. You completed all the process for buying the property. Now, you got an information about the actual owner of the land who is not the person you are dealing with. The person you are dealing with is fraud and presented fake documents to you. If you do not get the information about the right owner, it would be a situation that all your fund invested in that property would go in vain. While considering about the owner, you should bear in mind that the owner should be, Realistic person.

Straight forward with words and consent.

Should have the free will to sell the property.

Should be a person with legal ownership right.

Now you might get the idea why it is important to know about the owner of the property. You should check the documents reliability again and again to evaluate the actual owner. There is a controversy where the actual owner is the person who currently owns the property. If anyone had right on the property previously and now claims to be his property that would not work legally. The investors in real estate properties also trade with the ownership, so change in ownership occurs rapidly. So you need to be careful for judgement about the owner of the property.

Motive for selling the properties The motive of the owner of the property should be evaluated before you buy the property. There might be some issue with the property. In real scenario, sometimes it can be found that owners sell of their properties to avoid some lacking in the properties. Imagine you were offered a property with lower price, fair location and solid background of the owner. Now you bought the property and realize that the property has an issue with sue by government. To avoid the issue the owner sold this property to you. Now you are in risk that the property will be confiscated which will result in loss of the total amount of investment.

Like legal complexities, tax issues, problems with documentations, issue about the traders, and many other issue might arise. You should avoid buying such properties which are involved with such issues and the owner does not clarify the motive for selling.

Risk

Risk is the major factor of consideration while making an investment decision. Here in the real estate properties, the risk is involved with the property. If the risk is greater, you should avoid to initiate the investment. I think you know about the risk factors which I already discussed in the previous chapter. The risk in the real estate might include: Market risk which might cause due to the unfavorable movements Asset risk depending on the structure, location, price Liquidity risk due to the lacking of buyer of the property Credit risk which might be a result of the due from the tenants.

Leverage risk because of the lack of borrowing source or rise in the interest rate in the market.

So these are the information that you should collect and consider about the investment. I suggest make a thorough research about the property that you want to buy. This is the preliminary step where you will get the overview of the investment.

Selecting your motive for the investment

Motive of the investment bears a great impact on the investment. Think of your own situation, if you want a regular income you will rent your property. But if you want capital gain on your property, you would trade your property with the potential buyers for the achievement of your funds. If you find yourself attracted to your motive but you're intimidated by how to execute it, that's ok. You still have time to learn. Just make a note of it for now. This kind of focused decision-making process helps you identify knowledge gaps that you need to fill as you go. Here are some vision or motive that you can use for making your investment decision.

∞ Regular income on your funds: You might want to make a regular income in the form of rent from your property. Your motive of the fund might change the decision about your investment plan. The example that I gave earlier about Mr. Roberto where I stated about his apartment buying and getting monthly rent from his property.

∞ Capital gain on your investment: There is a chance that you can invest for appreciation of your fund and grow it. Here you will trade with your property so that you can get the chance of selling your property when it gives you higher price. By selling on higher price you can grow your fund.

[NB: The capital gain is the excess amount or the positive difference between the buying price and selling price of an asset. The rent or other income that is not part of the capital is not deemed as capital gain.]

∞ Saving the capital or fund from being idle or reducing the cost of capital: This might seem complicated to you. Well this is a financial technique for covering the cost of your capital. Ask me what kinds of cost? Now think that you have €100000 in your hand which you are keeping in safe as cash. You might think that this capital will remain the same so there will be no loss with the capital. But think of the inflation or time value of money. With the inflation you fund will loss the value that it has today. Think that you can buy a ton of wheat but after a year or more time you won't be able to buy a ton of wheat with the same price because of the rise in price or inflation. Similarly today's €100000 is worth more than €100000 in future date. The value that you are losing by keeping your fund idle is the cost of your capital. To avoid such cost of capital, some investor just buy a property and hold it since the value of the property will adjust with the inflation and the value of the fund in the market. Moreover, the property will give a certain cash flow if he want to use it as rental property.

Selecting a market or targeting a market

The selection of a market is the process of choosing among several location or marketplace where you want to make your investment process. Since the opportunities and facilities differ depending on the type of market or area or region. So you need to choose the market where you can get the best opportunity for utilizing your fund.

Sometimes the price, rent, interest rate differs in different market which can affect your investment decision. I suggest you to select the market or the location of your investment which is near for you or easier for you to locate and communicate. This will allow you to interpret the market and get the proper information when requires. The most devastating point of selecting market in your local area that there you can visit the property in your own and check for the issue that arises with your property. These facilities would be easier if you choose the location or the market near to your home.

Select your investment criteria

The investment criteria is the process or strategy that you follow in your investment. The criteria of your investment follows your motive of the investment. Now depending on your motive of investment you need to select the criteria. For example, Mr. Roberto has the motive for making a regular income from his property. So he buys a rental apartment which gives to tenant for a regular rent payment. Now Mr. Roberto gets a monthly income which I already explain in the example. Now the criteria for the investing in real estate can be different depending on your motive. The amount of fund also varies depending on the criteria of the criteria of the investment. Under the criteria of your investment the two major selection comes. One is selection of your property and the other is targeting the number of property.

Selecting the property requires choosing the land, apartment, building that you are going to buy. For the selection you can consider your choice of the property or the consideration about any property which I already explained before. On the other hand your motive for the investment will drive you to select the number of properties. The number of properties depends on your amount of funds you want to invest. I suggest you to look at the portfolio and risk management chapter before selecting the number of property for your investment. Selecting the properties according to portfolio and diversification will allow you to minimize the risk of your overall investment and maximize your return from your investment.

Building your team for investment

The team of investment is the manpower that you are working with for the completion of the investment process. Now you might ask why a team? The answer is that, you cannot do these tasks alone. Or if you want to handle your investment alone and employ agency for managing and maintain your investment, it will not be a smart choice because by doing so you won't have control on the cost of your investment such as, the agency will incur more cost for the maintenance of your property, they will charge more from you, they might not handle them so carefully like you would do. Overall managing your investment with you choosing team is the best way that most of the expert suggest in this sector. Here are a list of person who can be selected for your investment team, I will also mention the preferred duty or task by the person.

Relatives such as brother, spouse, niece and others who can support give you company with making your decision and while visiting the place.

Business partner with whom you share your professional life can support you when you need either with financial help, or decisional help.

Mentors or advisors who gives you suggestion about investment can be your best team member. Selecting a trusted mentor is essential in this field.

Property manager who is currently handling a property is helpful since he would have the experience that can guide you to the best decision.

Lenders who is lending you fund for investment can also be your team member.

These particular persons can be the member for maintaining your properties.

Agent for handling the property and controlling the issues with documentations.

Guards, for protecting your property.

Electrician Plumber Technician Painter Contractor and several other persons who are required for the maintenance of your property.

Interfering with documentation process

One of the most complex task for the investment in the real estate property is the activities with the legal documents. Since the real estate is the business or trading of immovable properties, it requires a legal process by the law. The documents or paper of the properties are to be justified and transferred by law and regulation with the initiation of the governmental body. In some cases you need to go to the customs for the clearance of your taxation or other issues. The ownership of the property that you choose would take legal prove for the transfer. The documentation process of the property differs depending on the types of property and the laws and regulations of the state or country.

Initiating the deal of the properties or making the transfer

Now you after the above stage, you are in the final stage for your investment where you are in front of the owner of the property for the exchange of ownership or transferring the property. The ownership exchange takes place with the exchange of the legal documents and registering with your name since you cannot exchange or transfer the immoveable property, you need to transfer the ownership right. With the exchange of ownership, you will be able to use the property for your motive. You remember the motive that you selected for the investment? Now it is to imply the motive with your property. Either you can sell it, give to tenant for rent, give it to agent for using, lend it to business man for the commercial use and whatever the motive you use.

For the transfer of ownership the transfer of the price is the main thing that is required to give to the owner of the property. The fund or the capital that you invest is to be transferred in this stage. I have already show you the ways of selecting your fund on the first stage. The fund for the transfer might be in the form of down payment or total amount pay by cash. Most of the transfer takes place with cash or check or other funds transfer. I suggest you to initiate down payment system that will allow you to pay of the price with the return in future. On the first stage I show you about selecting the funds from the funds you have, now here I will show you some source of fund that you can use for paying the value of property.

Personal saving which I already told you before.

Selling the property in which you will pay the price by selling property to another party. This process requires the regular trading and client in hand or available for you.

Borrowing banks or financial institutions, or friends, or relatives which indicates investing with leverage.

Business partner who will assist you in your investment and funds transfer.

Availing the property for use

The property after you buy should be maintained for use. You can use the property for the motive that you selected before. For the rental use you need to repair the property to make it ready for your tenant. For making a resale or to commercial space you need to find out the client. For these tasks you need the team of your investment for repairing or maintaining the property and finding out the clients for your properties.

Continue with the process

The process I showed you can be continued with the motive of your investment. Think that you are holding your property and lending it to tenants and business purpose for commercial use. This will give you a regular return. So now you need to maintain your property and let the tenant use it for a rent. As long as you want you can hold the property. Here are certain policy that you can follow for the process of trading Buying a property with above process Rehabbing, repairing or maintaining them Giving to tenant for rent and Refinancing When you motive for selling them and making capital gain you can follow the process to find the potential client and sell the property for higher price than the purchase price. Thus the trading of property continues where you can follow the process above for each and every investment. The this scenario the process might be suggested is Buying a property with above process Finding out the customer or client Selling them and Refinancing for another property So these were the process or guidance for your investment in the real estate properties. Following these you can make your investment and gain from your investment.

Online investment procedure

Modern era is proficient with the use of technologies and Medias which makes our life easy and comfortable. In case of investment and business, investors in present days can handle their business operations from their homes with the help of communication intermediaries, like mobile, computers, internet, social media, and emails and so on. The online platform or the internet has connected the whole world in one virtual place. The investors in several area can check their investment and transactions via online media. The real estate market is not far behind from the online investment procedure. These days' investors can interact with the companies they are dealing with and interpret their investment process. The online platform connects the dealers and the investors where they can also gather their thoughts and activities about the market. The exchange process of the funds and rights to use ownership are also available in the virtual world. The advantage of the online investing process are easier than the actual investment process. You will also have the benefit of not going to the physical location rather you can do them form your home of office. The disadvantage is that you cannot observe the property as you would be able to observe with direct visiting the property and observing the market by being present physically. All you need to do is connect with the website that allows you for investing in real estate properties. Like in Italy, the organizations SDA Bocconi, Green-Acres.it allow the investors in Italy for initiating online investing activities.

Strategies for Investment

There are several ways for the real estate investment opportunities. The opportunities for your investment depends on the utilization of your strategies and your decision making ability about the investment. There are basic two strategy that you can follow for your investment in real estate.

Active Real Estate Investment: Like the name suggest. The active real estate investment refers to investing in real estate with the involvement of the investor. Elaborating the term we get that, the investor, while handling the properties with direct involvement i.e. direct buying and selling or lending of his properties, it comes under this term. I would like to give an example of this term. Such that Mr. Roberto who wants to buy an apartment. Goes to the owner and buys the property. After buying the property Mr. Roberto needs to modify the apartment as per requirement which is to be done by his involvement. Afterward, Mr. Roberto needs to find out the customer by himself whom he is going to lend the property. Moreover, all the activities from the starting to the end, the activities are done with the direct involvement of the investor in this type of investment.

Passive Real Estate Investment: From the previous example, you might get an idea about passive investment. Well, you are right, this is just opposite to the active style of investment. Some of the investors just want to maximize their return on capital. They don't want to be part of any complexity. So they might choose this type of investing style. Here the investors are required to choose the agents who are actively working with the real estate operations. Those agents will invest and manage your funds and properties according to your instructions. Now look again on the scenario of Mr. Roberto, where being an old person, Mr. Roberto does not want to involve in these complex activities of real estate. So he calls upon an agent who works with the real estate investment. Now Mr. Roberto instructs the agent to purchase an apartment of choice for Mr. Roberto and allow the apartment for rental use. Now the agent will do the tasks that Mr. Roberto would do with the active involvement in the investment like maintaining the properties, repairing, finding clients and users, and other formalities. Of course, the agent will charge a commission. But here Mr. Roberto just having a benefit from the investment on the properties with the lower complexity of being involved in these activities.

Learning outcome of this chapter

From the evaluation and determination of the investment process and strategies you will be able to: Realize about the funding source and techniques Collect the information about the property and investment Evaluate the property value Interfere with documentation Make a target about market and profitability of investment and work accordingly.

Select the strategy for investing Select the property and make the investment.

Make profit or utilize the resources

CHAPTER FOUR: FINANCING, FORMULATING AND MANAGEMENT OF CAPITAL

From the previous chapter you already learn about the techniques and process of the investment in the real estate properties. Well from these chapter you are now able to invest and make money. But there are some tactics that the investors do while investing in the real estate properties. Suppose you are a general investor, and you invested your money in the real estate property. Now you are getting a regular payment from your fixed property by giving it for rent. If you look around, you will see some business persons or investors are making more profit or capital gain from their investment. In some cases some investors might get more return even if they invest less than you. This indicates that they are optimizing their investment whereas you are not in the process of optimizing your investment. May be you can grow more with the full utilization of your fund. The utilization of your fund requires the understanding of the funds and the return associated with the investment. Your source of capital and the management of the capital has a lot to do with your investment. Since the capital has a cost for managing and handling, you need to make sure that the cost is minimized which will increase the profit in the end. So, in this chapter I will show you the aspects of the capital that you should follow while collecting and managing your funds.

Source of Capital

There are several source of capital that you can use for your financing decision. If you are a businessman and working as a real estate investing company you can optimize two vast source for your capital financing source.

Private equity Private equity consist of the equity or capital that the owner or owners of organization provide in business firm. Generally private organizations or corporations has share that is owned by the individuals or the partners of the organization. Your company might be private organization or partnership organization. Your private equity and the source varies with the type of organization that you own. So here are the source of private equity depending on your organization type.

Private limited company: In the scenario of a private limited company, your firm's private equity will be the share of the owners that they provide as the capital for the organization.

Partnership organization: Similar to the private limited organization, the partners who owns the organization will provide the capital that is needed
Sole proprietorship firm: In case of your organization that you own, your private equity will be the amount that you invested in your organization as capital.

Public debt or financing While it is a public limited organization the financing of the capital or investment fund will be from the share or stock that is distributed among the general investors. In public limited firms the share that is distributed is the ownership right to the public where the investor who buys the shares, are the owner of the company. But don't think that private organization cannot borrow from public. There are also some opportunities for the private organization to collect funds from public via several means. Some of the source of public debt are shown below: Common stock or ownership share: The ownership share can also be shared among the public which I mentioned on the previous paragraph. The but you need to know that not only the public sector has the opportunity for distributing share among public, private limited corporations are also allowed to collect fund from public share. In public Limited Corporation most of the capital are distributed among the public for investment. But in private Limited Corporation less than 50% share can be distributed to public for investment. Minimum 51% of the total issued capital has be in private holdings. The rest can be distributed to public.

Bonds: Bonds are the debt paper that allows the investors to invest in the issuing company for a fixed and regular income. The principal amount of the investment will be given to the investor or holder at the maturity of the bond. It is a popular debt instrument which you can issue on the market for general investor to invest. The investors will invest in bond and pay your company with their funds which you will use and make profit. For the investment the issuing company has to pay a fixed interest rate on the bond. The bond acts like a loan from the public. The difference with loan is that with bond issue you can collect a huge amount from the market. With the issue of bond in the market you can collect your desired funds for investing in the real estate property Debenture: Like bond, debenture is another debt instrument which allows you to collect funds from the market. The difference with bond is that, debenture is a medium short term debt instrument which is not secured or backed by asset on the other hand bond is secured and backed by asset of the organization which issues the bond. With debenture, you can collect your capital or funds for the investment.

NB: Debt instruments are those commercial paper which can be used for collecting debt or managing debt. The debt instrument in the market are issued by the companies in the money market and capital market for collecting long term, short term and medium term loans.

Forwards: Forward is a contract for buying and selling a certain asset in a fixed future date with a fixed price or rate of exchange. The investors can collect their desired funds and reserve for the future in the form of future contract.

Options: Option is another contract which gives the holder of contract the right to sell or buy a certain asset. The investor of real estate market can sell some of the asset to other investors for the collection of funds. You can also make the transaction within a predetermined period which allows you collect funds from the sale of asset that you want to sell.

Swap: Swap is another contract like the forward and option. In this contract the parties are contracted for transferring a certain value among themselves for a certain period. These contracts are deemed as financial derivatives interfering with the transaction and giving advantages to the buyer and seller of properties or assets.

Futures: Future is another contract for transacting in the future which allows the holder of the contract to exercise the contract whenever he wishes to within the given time. The different with the forward contract is that the forward contract occurs at the end of the contract on a fixed time. Here the time has a limit and the occurrence of the transaction is dependent on the holder of the contract.

So these are the sources that allows you to deal with the public and collect funds from them. Most of the collection of funds is deemed as loan for you which you need to pay after a certain period.

Besides the private equity and public offering, there are several sources of your funds for investing in the real estate properties. Now the above two sources were on the perspective of the organizational view. Now think that you are a single investor, who just enter into the market and make your investment. So, here I will show you the types of funds that you can use for your investment.

Personal savings: As an investor, probably you have some funds which you can employ in the investment. Personal savings is the first thing that you can optimize for your investment. From the example I gave you several times before, Mr. Roberto, had his most of the investment funds from the savings that he saved from the salary of his job. Similarly if you have amount of savings, you can get them and invest in the real estate property. No matter what the amount is, you should not hesitate to go for your investment. All you need to do is separate your funds and keep the funds that you need for other things and invest the funds that are available for investing. This will give you the starting of the journey in this sector.

Borrowing: Borrowing or lending from your friends and relative is another major source for your capital for investing. You can call upon your friends or relatives who got some funds available and remain idle, you can borrow some amount from them and employ the amount in realizing the funds.

Loans: Loans are the ways of collecting funds from the sources in exchange for a certain interest payment. Loans can be collected from banks or certain persons who are willing to give loans. The loan requires a certain payment of interest. Some loans are backed by the property or mortgage while some loans might be just allowing the funds and paying off the debt amount. The source of loans can be different such as Commercial banks Loan brokers

Life insurance companies Financial loan providers Mutual savings banks Mortgage: Mortgage is another process of loan or borrowing which is backed by an asset or property. In mortgage scenario, if you want to get some funds from mortgage providers you need to put something valuable, like asset or properties that have certain value comparable with the loan or borrowed amount. You will be provided with the funds only after the submission of the property or the legal documents of the property. You will be given back with your property when you pay off the borrowed or loan amount. Like loans, mortgage can also be collected from banks, mortgage brokers and financial institutions.

Pension funds: The pension funds is the fund that the government pay to the retired job holder till a certain maturity or death. If you get some pension funds, you can save the amount of pension funds and invest them in real estate. Most of the people use the money from their pension fund for a capital expenditure like establishing business, buying properties, investing in business, building home apartments and so on. In this regard, you are required to invest your funds from pension in the real estate property.

REITs: I have already explained this term before in the second chapter which you might already know about. The collection of the funds using the REITs is a term that is most common in the real estate. The REIT is an organization that is in control of the investments in real estate properties such as buying, monitoring, executing, finding clients, collecting rents and so on. The REITs act as an agent for the investors. Not all investors are able to invest in large property alone. To buy a property like a house, land, or apartment it takes large amounts, which seems tough for some investors who can give their investment fund to REIT. REIT collects funds from several investors and invest in real estate properties for the investors and maintains the procedures of investment. It acts as mutual funds that distribute the profit after a certain period but it is not mutual fund. The main motive of this organization is to allow all the investors to have the opportunity to invest in real estate properties. The organization also reduces the complexity of the tasks related to real estate properties.

Credit unions: Another major source for funds to invest is credit unions that are available almost in every financial market. These unions provides the loan and credit to the borrower with certain regulations of their funds. You can opt for the credit from these union available in your local financial market.

Individual investors: There are several investors in the market who are ready to invest their funds. You can take advantage of the individual investors available in the market by borrowing from them or investing with them in which scenario they will provide you funds for investment, and with your fund the amount will greater for investing in larger properties. Sometimes the investors lends money for a certain profit or interest on their lending. You need to pay the interest from the profit you made from the investment.

Foreign funds: The funds from foreign investors are also the source for your investment capital. The foreign investors are reluctant about the market in your locality. While some foreign investors come in your city and try to invest, they won't be able to interact with the market as you can do. So the foreigners always trust someone who will support them with their investment. You can be the person to support them and use their funds for investment. Your profit from their funds will be depending on the contract that you enter with the investors.

Government association: There are some association by governments in each economy for helping the investors of the economy to invest and contribute to the economic activities. The more investment the more contribution to production and consumption which enhances the economic activities. The association helps the investors with the opportunities to collect funds, ideas, suggestions about investment. The association by government allows you funds for mortgage, property or with other conditions.

Accumulation of Capital

After the collection of the capital from different sources you are required to accumulate your funds for investment. Well, the term capital accumulation means to gather the funds from different sources and make it ready for the investment. The motive of the accumulation of capital is to maximize the amount of investment by gathering funds from different sources. Suppose you have your funds in different area. Like some of your funds are in banks deposit, some in savings accounts, some are in stock market, some are lent to friends. Now you realize investing in real estate will increase the value of your funds rather than the present scenario. So you are collecting your funds by withdrawing funds from banks, from depository investment, from friends, and other sources where you kept your funds. Gathering them you got a total amount which seems larger than individual sources. This is the process of accumulation of funds.

Cost of Capital

The cost of capital refers to the cost or expense that you need to incur for your capital. Suppose, you took a loan from bank for your investment so you need to pay a certain interest for the loan or capital. This payment or expense that you are paying to bank is a cost for your capital. If you have capital, you will have to incur a certain cost. Now, a question might arise why you need to pay cost of your own funds that is in your hand or what would be the cost of capital that you never borrowed from anyone. It's totally yours so, you are thinking that no cost are arising with your capital. Let's break out the term. The cost of capital is not just the interest or the expense that you are paying for your capital. It also refers to the factor that cause a reduction to your capital. If you keep your funds idle, there will be reduction in value due to inflation or the value of your fund will not be the same in future. The value that your fund losses is the cost for your funds. Similarly you might lose your capital while maintaining your fund without investing in any asset. Remember currency or money is liquid asset which changes its form and value. That is why most of the funds holder wants to keep their capital safe with fixed asset investment.

Return on invested capital

Return on your invested capital is the process of defining your ability of investing funds in the efficient asset that generates expected returns. It is represents as a rate or ratio based on the capital invested. It reflects how much worth the invested capital is. The return on capital invested is the indicator of profitability of the investment since it is compared to the cost that you are paying to the creditors or sources of funds. Now, if you are paying an average cost of 10% on your capital your standard return on the investment should be more than 10% which will give you the profit over the cost. If the cost of your capital is more than the return on invested capital, you will have to incur loss on your capital.

[NB: Average cost of capital is measured with a standard costing method which is represented as the WACC stands for Weighted Average Cost of Capital. In this process the cost of each sources of capital are considered along with the weight of the portion of capital which represents the perfect and standard cost for the capital.]

Learning Outcome of this Chapter

From this chapter you will be able to understand the following What source you can use for funding your capital?

Which are most useful source for you?

You will be able to accumulate capital from different sources.

You can make the best use of the investment and make profit.

You will be able to minimize the cost for your capital.

You will be able to compare your investment with the cost and optimize your return.

CHAPTER FIVE: GENERATING PROFIT FROM INVESTMENT AND OPTIMIZING FUNDS

From earlier discussion, you got the reason why your funds should be invested. Investment is the process of employing your funds or capital for the generation of positive return. The return from your investment can be in the form of capital gain or interest or profit. The most desirable income from investment is the regular profit count. Unlike other investment investing in the real estate property can get you a regular income. By investing in rental properties, you can get rental payment per month or year. While if you want a capital gain from your investment, you will also get capital gain or growth in your capital by engaging in trading of real estate properties. Real estate properties give you the opportunity for gaining your desired return from your investment. Well you have got the idea about the real estate investment and making profit from investment. Now, in this chapter I will show you the way you can utilize your return. Suppose you have invested in real estate properties and gaining a return of your desire, but some other investment is getting more return with same line of investment? How? The answer of the question lies in the optimization of funds. The funds that you invested can be optimized by the observation of the investment scenario in the market. There are certain techniques for the optimization of funds. Here I will show you some measures which you can follow to optimize your fund and make the right use with your funds.

Motive of investment and the measures that you can take

The first thing that comes in this process is the selection of motive for your investment which I stated many time in the previous chapter. But, just selecting the motive is not enough for your investment. The motive that you are selecting should be more relevant to the investment.

Imagine Mr. Roberto have invested in two apartment at the same time €300000 in each apartment. And you invested €100000 in a cottage. Now with rental income Mr. Roberto gets €40000 every month from his apartments. Here if you think you can also get €40000 monthly income and select your motive to get that much amount from your little investment your motive for the investment would not be relevant.

So your motive for your investment should be relevant to your funds. And the matter of risk tolerance comes with the motive. Your motive should also be relevant to your risk tolerance. There is proverb goes "No risk, no gain". The proverb is modified in the business as 'more risk, more gain'. So, you have to incur more risk for gaining more profit. Or I can express it like more profit requires more risk. So you should have the tendency of bearing a certain risk for your investment depending on your motive.

Decision regarding your investment in different asset and choosing the asset

The decision of investment are always dependent on the investors. As an investor it is you who takes the decision about your investment. Of course there is lot of opportunity to take suggestion about the investment. But the investment and the profitability of investment depends upon your decision. Since there are a lot of choice regarding the investment, your decision of the investment requires the choosing of the properties among them. Your decision reflects your ability about the investment and utilization of funds. The most devastating point of the decision is that the investment appraisal process in the decision depends upon you.

Suppose you get an opportunity to buy an apartment with lower price say at €80000 while most of the apartment in the market are selling at an average price of €150000. So you might think that buying that apartment would give you more return. Here comes a challenge of decision. You have to collect the information about the apartment I stated on chapter three. After the collection of information about the apartment you realize that the apartment has an issue with the court. So the value of the apartment has decrease. With this situation you would be in the risk of losing value after buying the apartment. Also there would be some trouble with finding tenants for that apartment.

So, investing with lower cost and higher return does not always mean that you have taken a better decision. Taking risk gives you a better return. But all the risks are not affordable. You have to initiate the risk that you can tolerate or you should employ your funds in risky property which you can meet with your back up fund.

[NB: Backup fund means to have some amount safe for your investment. If you incur loss, or reduce the amount of funds from your investment, the funds that you use for covering the amount is called the backup fund. Most of the organization keeps their backup funds as the reserve fund.]

The decision or the choice of asset should be made with the asset. In case of the real estate investment, there are several properties that you can invest. Not all the property are for you. The asset or property might differ depending on the motive or funds available in your hand. Funds are always limited. So with the limited resources, you have to select the funds that would fill the motive or desire of your investment. The most suggested phenomena in selection of asset is the making of portfolio. The portfolio of your asset will give you the chance to maximize the return as well as minimize the risk associate with the assets or properties. Here are some details about making portfolio.

Portfolio investment Portfolio is the investment procedure where you divide your amount of funds into parts and invest them in different assets. With the emergence investment on the market, you are able to purchase and sell the several asset of your choice. By dividing your asset in parts and investing in different assets you will be able to maximize your potential return. The probability of return rises and risk probability reduces.

Suppose you have €200000 in your hand which you have invested in a property which will give you a monthly return of €10000. In this scenario if there is any unexpected event with the property that the property losses its value, you will loss the total amount of investment. Now think again that you invested asset A €50000, asset B €60000, asset C €40000 and in assed D €50000. These asset will give you a monthly return consecutively €3000, €4000, €2500 and €2500. So now look at the scenario. Now look at the scenario, the return of total amount will be (€3000+€4000+€2500+€2500) €12000. Additionally if any asset goes in vain, other assets will be the backup of the loss.

One of the most effective ways of utilizing your fund is the formation of a portfolio. With a portfolio, you can maximize your return and minimize your risk with the efficient formation of the portfolio.

Diversifying your assets considering the geographic location.

Not just making portfolio will allow to reduce the risk associated with the investment. Diversification is another term which you need to know and imply while making portfolio of investment. The diversification will allow you to work with every single asset for the reduction of risk. Another phenomena that you are going to follow is the location of your property which you can select from different place.

<u>Diversification</u> Well, this term might seem unfamiliar to you. This is a financial term. If you have an understanding of financial terms, you might hear about this, but if you are not, then this short introduction about diversification is for you to understand the term. The term refers to the technique of selecting and investing in the assets or properties which minimize the risk of a portfolio of certain assets or properties. You might ask why diversification? While making a portfolio makes a reduction of your risk. Well, the portfolio making is for minimizing the overall risk of your fund. In some scenarios, the risk might not be less, while you are expecting a high return portfolio you might incur some risk on your overall portfolio. The formation of a portfolio works on the overall risk related to the investment. But the diversification works with an individual security risk. Now diversification of your real estate property investment is for the motive of managing the risk of every property you are investing in. Now before making your portfolio you should consider diversifying your properties and incur the less risk as much as possible.

Selecting the same location for your properties will give you the benefit of visiting all the properties at the same time. But selecting properties in different location will minimize the risk of area based problem. Such as think that you have your lands, apartments, house in the same side of your town. Now if a flood hits the town all your property will be at stake and you won't be able to get return from those property. Think again that if the property were in different paces there might be a chance that some asset or any single asset would not affected with the flood. Like flood there might be several other occurrence with your property. So here in this part I will show you the process of diversification and the property selection according to the geometric location of property. The process includes three basic stages. I am going to point out those stages.

1. Geographic Diversification: The geographic diversification is the way of diversifying the asset or property in different location. For the real estate market the geographical diversification implies the diversification the properties in different countries in greater sense. If you have enough funds for entering in the greater market rather than the local market, you can choose to invest in the properties which are located in different countries of the world.
2. Management Style Diversification: The management diversification involves the process of adding value to the investment and enhancing the growth potential. Under the management style diversification the main aspects that comes under consideration are the value and growth of your property or investment. The way of management diversification can reduce the volatility in your investment portfolio.
3. Market capitalization: Market capitalization refers to the capital portion of your investment in the market. It reflects the weight of your investment comparing to the market. The reflection would be on the total investment including small, large, medium properties where you invest. It also considers the thing about the market stock of your organization.

The plan for the your investment

Of course you have the plan for investment in the real estate that is why you are initiating and reading this book to gather some knowledge about the real estate market. You have plan for the investment and making profit from the investment. But is your plan efficient enough for performing as per your expectation? If your answer is yes then you are efficient planner, if your answer is no, then you must revise your plan and include missing factor in your plan. The fundamental consideration for planning about your investment is the cost, return, and risk, period of investment, stability, and tax consideration and so on.

Monitoring and controlling your investment

This are the act of a manager. In this scenario you will act as the manager of your fund. In your investment the funds that have invested in your property should be monitored and managed for further income from that property. As long as you hold the property you need to take care of the property. Suppose you bought an apartment, this is not enough to get the profit from that apartment. The management process of an investment requires the tasks that are done till the selling of that apartment to another investor or owner. Within this mean time you have to repair that apartment, find tenants, maintain the apartment so that there would not be any harm to the property, making it suitable for the tenant, collecting rents and so on. All these activities come within the management of funds i.e. the monitoring and controlling of the investment. You should be careful while managing your investment. The within the management of your investment, the observation of the profitability and productivity of your investment also comes. The management of your investment is a continuous process in which the profitable investment properties are monitored and handled throughout the life of the investment properties. While there is a negative return from the investment, the management of the investment requires that the investment in that the activities regarding the properties are changed for turning the negative return into positive return if not possible, then the investor should get back the amount of investment fund from that property by selling them off and invest in another property. This process continues with the profitable investment property and in case of loss making property, the funds are invested in another property by the investors.

An example can be given where, Mr. Roberto bought an apartment at €300000. The apartment gives a return of €10000 per month which seems lower than other apartments of similar type. So Mr. Roberto finds out the reason for the lower rent of that apartment which is the location of the apartment. So, now since he can't change the location of that apartment, he changes his investment. He sells of that apartment and invest in other apartment where he will get €20000 per month.

So the management of the investment in the real estate property should be interacted by the investors and continue with the investment.

Reviewing Your Portfolio and Rebalancing for a Better Investment Performance

So you have got the idea of the portfolio formation of your investment by including the properties in your investment portfolio. But your portfolio always changes depending on the fluctuation of market price and demand of the properties. So what should you do? You should always update the portfolio according to the requirements of the portfolio. The reviewing your portfolio requires the following steps to be done by you. Such as Assessing your portfolio how you distributed the parts of your funds.

Determining the state of your properties Evaluate the state of the properties on international perspective.

Rechecking the liquidity state of the asset Make the change where needed.

Rebalancing is another term which you need to understand for making the change in your portfolio. It refers to aligning or rearranging the investments of your portfolio accordingly for the optimization of the investment portfolio. Rebalancing requires the ability to interact with the financial process. The rebalancing of your portfolio should be made by updating the investment amounts in such a way in which the profitable investment would be in the first line of choice and the lower profitable investment should be in the last line of choice.

An example can make it clear to you. Imagine Mr. Roberto made his investment in one apartment, one cottage, a land and a commercial building by employing amount consecutively €80000, €100000, €150000, and €170000. From those investments Mr. Roberto got return as the rent consecutively €10000, €12000, €16000 and €18000. After a year the rent from the commercial building has been reduced. So Mr. Roberto reviewed his portfolio investment and change it. He sold the Commercial building and invest that in other assets. Now Mr. Roberto has reformed his portfolio with two apartment at €150000, a cottage at €100000, a land at €150000 and a new plot of land at €90000.

So these were the techniques you can follow for reviewing your portfolio and rebalancing your investment. The rebalancing of your investment motives for the change in your funds invested for avoiding the investment that cause a reduction or loss to your portfolio as well as adding the profitable investment to your investment portfolio.

Learning Outcomes from this Chapter

From this chapter you will learn the following things: You will be able to make a perfect plan for your investment.

You will be able to make the portfolio and diversify your properties for each investment.

You will be able to take the steps to minimize the risk and optimize the return from your portfolio You will be able to conclude about the portfolio You will be able to manage the funds of your portfolio by changing the amount and rebalancing.

CHAPTER SIX: SELECTION OF PROPERTY

For the investment process in the real estate organization, you need to choose your property accordingly which best suits your investment. For the investment procedure, the most challenging and hard task is the choice of property or the selection of property among several properties available in the market. While looking at the huge number of properties available in the market for you, you might get confused with the properties. So what you need to do is interpret them with a preferable selection model or criteria. Following a selection model or criteria will allow you to choose the best options among several options in your hand. In this chapter I will show you the procedures for selecting the best property for your investment. At first let's take a look at the points why you should use the property selection model or criteria. The selection of property for the investment in real estate properties are done with four major stages.

1. Determining the requirements for your investments and properties.

2. Finding out the properties that match your requirements

3. Focusing on the each matched properties and evaluate the result

4. Listing with priority and select the top

Here in this portion, the activities under each stages are described below:

Determining the requirements for Your Investments and Properties

On the first stage of property selection model, you need to set the requirements of your investment. On this stage you need to point out the requirement or characteristics of the properties that you want to avail in your property. For pointing out the requirements of your investments you can find the answers of the following questions: What would be the size of investment?

Under this question the size of investment or the amount of fund will be evaluated. As an investor you need to determine how much fund you can invest. Depending on your fund the property will vary. Suppose Mr. Roberto had €300000 in hand, but he wanted to have a commercial building that costs €600000 for selling. So, here in this scenario Mr. Roberto needs to find the property which suits his fund.

How can you access your investment?

After you make the investment you need to access the property, visit them and manage them for getting your return. The management of your property and the activities for getting the return from your property are to be answered in this question. Answering these you will understand the tasks and activities that you will have to go through. With these answers, you can evaluate how you need to work what measures you can take for making profit from your investment. Example of these tasks are, the process of documentary and transfer of property, maintaining the property, finding out the tenants or clients.

What would be your communication mode?

Communication system for visiting your property physically will help you to perform the activities for management and control. Keeping communication with the property will let you control and maintain the property. So you need to consider your communication method for the property.

What would be your motive for investment?

The main factor about your investment is your motive for the investment. The motive for investment about which I already explained in previous chapter is the most important thing that drives your investment strategy, quality and overall investment decision. Under this question, you need to consider which types of return you are expecting from your investment, what types of funds you want to manage with your investment. Moreover the objectives or goals that you are looking for from this investment will come under this question.

What would be the location of your property?

The location, another major phenomena for your property that drives the value and the demand of your property. The location of your property should be selected in such a place where you can visit, control your property as well as have competitive advantages from your with your investment in that property. It is the location that decides the demand for your property. With more demand of your property the rent or price for your property goes higher. Now imagine again that you got an offer to buy an apartment. You bought the apartment and did not even visit the location and did not even get any information about the location. And after making the purchase you can't find any client or tenant for your apartment. Now, after intervention on the matter you see that the location of the apartment is far away from the locality for which no one is getting interested to buy or rent that apartment.

How far it will be from your location?

Most of the expert will suggest you to select the location near to you. Meaning that the location of the property should be in your town where you can go and visit with less time spend in communication. It also have been explained before on this book. So I think you got the idea of the location. Under this consideration you need to evaluate how far the location of the property is from your home.

Will the property be in rural area?

Some investors initiate their investment in rural area where the price of the property are lower than the urban area. In most cases the organizations or corporations takes this types of initiatives for minimizing their cost of properties. Managing individual properties in rural area would be tough. So it is up to you where you are going to invest.

What type of infrastructure your property will possess?

The structure or the infrastructure that your property should possess should be evaluated under this question. The structure of the property includes the size of the land, apartment or whatever property you are going to invest in. In case of building or apartment the room numbers, floors and other structural definition should be defined under this question.

Finding out the Properties That Match Your Requirements

With the requirements that have been stated on this chapter, you should select the properties form the market among several choice of properties. The developing world will give you several opportunities for investing in real estate properties with variety of choice of the properties. The properties includes lands, buildings, houses, commercial places, and several other immovable properties. In the market where the real estate properties are traded, you will see a lot of properties that are being traded will be listed. Under the property matching and selecting the list of properties you can consider the following factors about the property.

The size of the apartment or land or house.

Space on the location Communication method to the location Structure of the property Rooms size Number of rooms available in that property.

Style or design of the property Utilities used in that property Layout of the land or block From the observation of the following things, you are required to choose the properties that matches your requirements. For the matching of the requirements you should check the price, location, capacity, and structure of the properties and make your own list of properties which you can evaluate and determine profitability. Remember one thing, never judge a property too quickly with just overview of the property. There are several matter of consideration before the decision of investment. The list of the properties are to be made for further evaluation process of the requirements and information about the properties will be collected.

Focusing on Each Matched Properties and Evaluate the Result

In this stage of evaluation, the list of properties are to be evaluated. The evaluation of property have already mentioned earlier. For the evaluation of properties, you need to justify each and every property from the list you have made with your matching requirements. The list consists of the properties of your choice. So here each and every property is valuable for judgement. The final selection of the property requires the fulfilment of the motive of the investment. The motive of the investors can be varied which was explained before. Now we assume most of the investors invest depending on the best profitability. For the evaluation of the profitability of each property, you can consider the following things.

Price: The first information that all the investor considers is the price of the asset. Most probably you would also even if I would not suggest you here. The price or the trade cost is the main indicator about your investment. You should get the information from real source. Assume Mr. Roberto trying to buy an apartment so he heard from a person about the apartment price. But the person he asks does not know the actual price of the apartment, so the person gives a wrong information. Or in some scenario the person might motive to make a fraudulent act with Mr. Roberto. So these might be conflicting for Mr. Roberto. He should seek for the seller or the current owner of the apartment. So the source of the information about the price should be clear and authentic.

Return on investment: Return on your invested capital is the process of defining your ability of investing funds in the efficient asset that generates expected returns. It is represents as a rate or ratio based on the capital invested. It reflects how much worth the invested capital is. The return on capital invested is the indicator of profitability of the investment since it is compared to the cost that you are paying to the creditors or sources of funds. Now, if you are paying an average cost of 10% on your capital your standard return on the investment should be more than 10% which will give you the profit over the cost. If the cost of your capital is more than the return on invested capital, you will have to incur loss on your capital.

Risk: Risk is the major factor of consideration while making an investment decision. Here in the real estate properties, the risk is involved with the property. If the risk is greater, you should avoid to initiate the investment. I think you know about the risk factors which I already discussed in the previous chapter. The risk in the real estate might include: Market risk which might cause due to the unfavorable movements Asset risk depending on the structure, location, price Liquidity risk due to the lacking of buyer of the property Credit risk which might be a result of the due from the tenants.

Leverage risk because of the lack of borrowing source or rise in the interest rate in the market.

So these are the basic information that you should collect and consider about the investment for evaluating the investment. I suggest to make a thorough research about the property that you want to buy. This is the preliminary step where you will get the overview of the investment. Remember you should not skip any investment from evaluation. The evaluation of the factors will show you the result about the profitability of the investment.

Listing with Priority and Selecting the Top Properties

After evaluating the properties with the consideration of profitability. You are required to make a list again. Here in this list the properties should be listed and shorted according to the profitability. From the list of profitability, you are required to select the properties that meets the demands of your investment.

So these were the selection of properties through which you can select your property from various choice of property from the market. It is the most important thing for you to select the best and profitable property which will appreciate your fund and achieve the motive for your investment.

Learning Outcome of This chapter

The property selection model or criteria will teach you the following things
You will be able to select your motive and define the property that you need to invest.

You will be able to evaluate the properties that are currently selling on the market.

You will be able to conclude about the properties and compare them with each other You will be able to select the better one for your investment
Overall, you will be able to make your investment efficient to meet your goal.

CHAPTER SEVEN: INCREASING YOUR PROPERTY RETURN

After the selection of properties from the market which is a challenging task for you, you should now meet the task which can increase the profitability of your properties. Here in this stage you need to work with every single asset. If you are able to make a positive return from your property, you can also add value to your property. Adding value to your property or getting more profit from your investment requires some process and procedures. These process might seem same to the process that I have included in the optimization process of investment. Well the investment optimization process can be applied in all types of investment while these process are for your properties to increase the value and increase the return from your property. So let's break out the process.

Pay the Interest Fast

You should pay the interest on time. When it incurs with the capital you should pay it. If you keep it due it will be increased with the reserve of interest by the flow of time. Again some loans possess the compound interest rate. So if you don't pay interest amount they will also consume more interest for you to pay in the future date. The minimization of interest cost gives you the opportunity to contribute to the profit of the property in the future. Another factor of the interest payment is that the interest of loans are tax deductible. So with the interest payment you can show cost more and deduct our taxable income. I suggest you to take loans for your investment. There is a provisions of deduction of taxable income while you have loans incurred in your investment.

Minimize Your Cost

There several types of cost that you need to face with your property. The costs of the properties can reduce the profit. So you need to consume the cost as less as possible. The cost including the maintenance of property, communication, repairing, documentation *etc.* should be conducted in the manner that reduces the overall cost. Notice that interest of loans also comes under the cost of investment. For which you need to take loans from the source where the interest rate is lower. The lower interest will consume low interest cost. You also need to follow the interest payment strategy stated above.

Invest in the Flexible Property

The flexible property means the properties that are easy to trade in the market. With the flexible properties in the market you would be able to change your investment property whenever you want. If you realize the property return is not meeting your expectation, you can make change to your investment. The flexible property are in top priority of investors, so you don't need to face trouble while reselling the asset to other investors.

The Prediction of Future and Manage Things Accordingly

Future is always uncertain. But in some scenario, you can assume what is going to happen with the matter you are considering by the analyzing the factors. In your investment of properties, you need to analyze them and predict the future. Since you are new in the market, you might have trouble with your assumption about the future. So you can take suggestion from the experienced investors or professional in the market. I suggest you to check the activities of the investors and observe how they are reacting to the market trends and taking their steps assuming the future of market situation. You need to analyze the market as well as the singe property for the assumption and prediction.

Utilize Your Team for Investment and Make It Efficient

The team you build for performing the activities of investment should be efficient enough for interacting the market activities and influence the investment to move towards its goal. The members of the team should be selected depending on the characteristics and the requirements of the property and the investment. You take the decision and the members of your team make them happen. So select the team that best suits you.

Finding out the Best Tenant or Client

The best tenant or client is the one who consumes your property and contribute to the positive return. The tenants who gives you more price might not be the best, the best tenant is that person who handles and use your property carefully and manages them in the smooth manner.

Do Not Depend on the Agent for Your Investment

As a new investor you might employ an agent for investing and managing the investment. But my suggestion for you is that if you go to an agent for investing do not depend fully on the agent. You can take help in some activities or get suggestion and do the task on your own. The reason for this is that if you just employ your fund to an agent and the agent manages your investment, you won't learn anything about the investment and you will have to employ the agent for long. But in case you do the tasks and activities by yourself, you will have experience. Besides not all the agents are trusted in the market and they have a charge which you have to pay. The charge to the agent is a cost for you which you need to minimize for the generation of profit.

Learning Outcomes of This Chapter

The main things that can be learned from this chapter are: You will be able to know about the interest rate and facing the cost.

You will be able to manage your fund You will be able to interpret the market trend and assume the future You will be able to select the property that best suits you Overall you will be able to make an efficient investment and investment decision regarding your investment.

CHAPTER EIGHT: FUNDAMENTAL CONSIDERATION BEFORE INVESTING

Major things for consideration before investing

Profitability

The thing that first comes into consideration is profitability. Let's begin from the first with the question, why you invest in a real estate? Most probably the answer will be for making a profit and using the funds rather than keeping them idle. For the profitability of the investment in the real estate market, you will assume the profit of several investment and make your investment on the property which will add value to your funds according to your desire. Your assumption might not always be true about the future movements of funds. So what you need to do is to compute or evaluate them with the technical approach which we had discussed in the evaluation part. With the evaluation of your investment, you can look at the whole picture of your investment. After checking out the profitability of your investment you can go for investing in the property you have selected.

Risk

With previous chapters, I already show you the way which bears the risk of the investment. The risk in real estate investment is that the person you are entering in contract or trading with properties might be fraud which arise the conflict situation for recovering the invested amount or there might be problem with the property that you are buying for which you might not get the value you want in the future. While investing, you should consider the risk factor which is related to your property. While investing, if you invest in just one type of property, this risk might incur in your investment. Investing in a portfolio with a different property will reduce your risk factor. The government properties or the properties involved with the governmental activities possesses the most safety as investing in the real estate market.

Growth

Growth of your investment means rising or increasing your funds. The value that investment should be increasing day by day. There are some investors who seek the growth of funds for their long term future prospects. While some other investors might want to have a short term return. Also, there are some investors who want both. Your investment decision might be changed when you think about the expectation of the future. Let's make it clear to you. You are an investor. You have enough funds which you want to invest in the real estate property. You are expecting your funds to raise and you are so interested in regular income in the form of rent. So now you can invest your fund on apartment which will give you rent per month or year. Now think the opposite, you are expecting a capital gain or growth of your funds, so now you might choose the trading or transaction of the properties in the market.

Liquidity

In the section of portfolio, I have shown you about the liquidity motive of a portfolio. While you need more liquid asset you should invest in those properties which are highly tradable in the market. Almost all the properties are traded in the market, here highly tradable indicating that your property will be such kind which has a higher demand in the market and by selling the properties you would not lose any value. Say, while you have a land property in the commercial area of the town, you can sell it at the market when you want, most of the time while selling you don't have to sell it on discount or lower price.

Diversification

Well, this term might seem unfamiliar to you. This is a financial term. If you have an understanding of financial terms, you might hear about this, but if you are not, then this short introduction about diversification is for you to understand the term. The term refers to the technique of selecting and investing in the assets which minimize the risk of a portfolio of certain assets. Now you might ask why diversification? While making a portfolio makes a reduction of your risk. Well, the portfolio making is for minimizing the overall risk of your fund. In some scenarios, the risk might not be less, while you are expecting a high return portfolio you might incur some risk on your overall portfolio. The formation of a portfolio works on the overall risk related to the investment. But the diversification works with an individual risk of your property. Now diversification of your property investment is for the motive of managing the risk of every property you are investing in. Now before making your portfolio you should consider diversifying your properties and incur the less risk as much as possible.

Tax

You probably know this term. Depending on your income from your investment, you have to spend some portion of paying the tax. You should always bear in mind that your income from the investment is taxable, so your income planning should be such which reaches your income goal from your investment even after paying the tax.

Suppose your income range is £100 and you are under 20% tax bracket, so you have to pay £20 as tax, which might impact on your income. Within this amount spending of £20 is not a less amount. But if your income gets £20000, you will have to pay £4000 as tax, this amount might seem same as per the previous, but think with £20000 profit, spending £4000 would not have that adverse effect on your income. With this amount, you will still have another £16000.

So the tax amount is a considerable fact before you make your investment. You should decide your investment amount so that the tax would not make any negative impact on your profit or income from your investment.

The Factors of Consideration before Investing

Similar to the above discussion, here are also some factors that are fundamental before you make your investment decision. I will shortly describe every factor here which will give you the idea of the facts.

Make sure to utilize your fund

Before your investment you should check is there any opportunity which you are missing? Is there any other way that can be used for optimizing your fund in a more efficient way? If so then you should rethink your investment decision.

Now think you are investing a certain amount on an apartment which gives €20000 return as rent from tenant. After investing you are realizing that you could get more return from another apartment with the same location and same investment. After investing it would be late to take back your investment and reinvest on a profitable apartment. And getting back invested funds within a few times would incur some cost of selling at less price than the purchase price.

So make sure you are taking the right decision about your investment. Not all investors can make the right decision. Those who are more efficient decision-makers are likely to be successful with their investment and make the right use of their funds.

Make your motive for your investment

Whatever the market goes, you should stick to your plan and your assumption. Do not go with the hype. Because there is no existence of an efficient market where you get the right information about the market. So your motive for your investment should be straight. Select what you want. As the previous discussion, it is you who decide what types of portfolio you form and which types of property you choose for your investment. All these theories, evaluation is to help you with your decision. The decision about the investment is yours. Your investment portfolio or individual investment depends on your motive. Also, the utilization of your fund depends on the motive that you have for your investment.

Make sure you are able to initiate the risk related to your investment

Investment in a real estate property is deemed as permanent income property. Although it trades with higher stability, it has also some risk. In fact, every investment that has returned has some potential risk more or less. While investing in properties, you should keep in mind that your fund is being used in immovable properties which is providing you the return which the by letting your tenants use them. The return that the tenant pays varies due to the characteristics of property and how the tenant will use your property. While using your property, there might be some default or another occurrence with your property. There are several examples like this. So you are giving your property to another person who will use it and give you a rent as your return from that property. So consider these things about the risk of investing. If you cannot bear such types of risk, the real estate investment market is not a place for you. Most of the investors take that risk and their risk is compensated while they get the return of their expectation. So the major suggestion for you is to "invest and manage the investment to achieve your goal about the investment."

Period of investment

Can you lend some money to your friends for a long time? Maybe yes or not. The investment decision is also dependent on such a question. Once you make the investment your fund will scroll around the market. There are several procedures to get back the investment amount before the maturity period, but this procedure hinders the achievement of the investment goals. So before investment think again if you can lend your fund until the invested period? This might change your investment decision or influence you to change the investment type. Suggestion for you is that you should select your investment portfolio depending on the type of property such that if you want your fund back within a short time you should avail the investment which is flexible in the market and you can sell them any time on the market with the relevant price within a shorter period. And if you can tolerate more time to get back your investment, then you can invest in fixed property and use it as rental property to generate profit. And if you tend to make an investment forever and utilize and raise your funds to grow, then the suggestion for you to avail whatever you feel comfortable with and be active on the market. With every type of property, you can avail every advantage that the market gives.

Recommendations for the new investors

If you are already an investor in the real estate market, then you might know the tactics for investing in a property market. With investing experience, investors get the market idea and tactics about the market and are able to make the decision about their investment. But this book is for the person who is new in this field. Being new, there is a possibility for an investor to make the wrong decision. So here are some suggestions and recommendations for them which will help them evaluate the market and prepare for investing in the real estate market. If you have read all the techniques, you might now understand the phenomena of the real estate market. So you think you are prepared, but just remember there are several investors like you who are falling due to their wrong decision about their investment. Now here are some attribution which might help you make the right decision about investment in the real estate market. These attributions might seem an individual's personal factors, but trust me, these works better in taking better decisions.

Manage your personal balance for investing

The first recommendation for you is the management of your personal funds. You might have a huge amount of funds. Not all of your funds would be available for investing. You might engage some of your funds for another use. Separate the investment fund that you want to invest in. This will help you with the planning of investment and income. You should not mix up your funds which are for another use with the funds that you kept for investing. Mixing up would result in conflict creation about investing. Managing your balance would also recommend that you should select the way of your investment plan and the fund's utilization plan. Also, you need to draw a road map that you will follow with your investment path. Say if you don't have any plan or management of your funds, you won't set the goal of the investment, thus the unplanned investment will result in losing your funds or incur a loss of your funds.

Make a comfortable decision

You should bear in mind that there are some conflicts of mind when you are not used to investing in the market. So make a comfortable zone which you won't feel tensed investing in the market. Make a habit then gradually improve your habit. Slowly you will be comfortable with your investment and investing decisions. The investors who are successful attempt to make more funds by investing more. You have to decide about the investment which feels comfortable for you.

Do not depend on single security for your expected income

In the portfolio, it has been concluded that you should make your investment in several assets, rather than an individual asset. Depending on individual property might give you a higher rate but with uncertainty about the individual property, you will end up losing most of your fund.

For instance take a consideration of example, where you chose 3 apartment with €8000, €9000, and €10000 return as rent. All the apartment with the same feature and same location. Now most of the new investors would invest in the apartment that gives rent of €10000.

In scenario one, you make your investment on the €10000 rent apartment. But after a certain period, the apartment gets burned. With this uncertainty you loss all your amount.

Now think about scenario two, you invested your funds in three apartments. So if one of the apartment gets burned, you will have the other two apartment to recover your invested amount. Although all your funds might not be recovered fully, you won't end up losing most of your funds like scenario one.

The investment in several assets is a fruitful method in which one security works as the backup of another security. Among several properties of the portfolio, there are more possibilities that some properties might generate a very positive return to cover the rest of the negative return.

Mixture of investment

While investing in a portfolio, you should consider that you have the properties of different types. Not only different properties but also check the properties belong to different locations. Because in some cases it is observed that within the same location line there would be influence of the market with price fluctuation. So if you include properties form different locations but from the same industry line, there would be a possibility that all your investment perform well or all of your investment be in vain. So diversify your investment with the opposite types of properties such that if one property outperforms, another will cover up the loss.

Back up on emergency

Among your funds for investment, keep some amount as back up in case of emergency needs. Not just emergency needs, sometimes investors have an opportunity but cannot avail of the opportunity due to scarcity of funds. So you need to keep some amount which would act as your back up on emergency and make the right use when the opportunity comes.

For instance, think that you made all your investments in a portfolio. After a certain period of investment, you have an opportunity to buy a property with higher return on the market available for you. But you don't have any funds available. So you cannot avail of the opportunity. Also, there would be so many situations where you might need some backup funds. So try to manage some portion of your funds keeps liquid for utilizing them on the emergency situation.

Make your personal balance

The balance of your investment consists of the accounts and records of your investments. You should maintain the balance of your investment funds so that you can assume and evaluate the performance of your investment.

Always update the balance with market trends and make your decision accordingly in relation to the market trends. Your balance of investment and the record of your accounts are helpful for your future prospects about investments.

Identify the misbehave and avoid fraud

Fraudulent activities can be everywhere. In the real estate market, there are several third parties working with investment. You should identify the fraud person related to investment and avoid them. Stick to the legal procedure of investment you will end up with a good result. Do not engage yourself with illegal activities regarding the market. This will take you to the fraudulent activities which are strictly prohibited by the market and the laws.

Standardization of investment

The standardization of your investment means to select the standard style of your investment, market observation, and evaluation. You should formulate your own standard about the market and your investment. Your investment and performance of investment show the standardization of your investment. Make the steps that are needed to maintain your standard.

Learning outcomes form this chapter

The last chapter of this book about the suggestion and recommendation for you. With this chapter: You will be able to evaluate the considerations of the major things before investment.

You will be able to make yourself ready for investment in the real estate market.

You will be able to become proactive investor.

You will be able to take an efficient decision about your investment.

CONCLUSION

Real estate investing rewards people who treat it less like a lottery ticket and more like a long game. By now, you've seen that success isn't built on secret tricks—it's built on clear goals, careful research, realistic numbers, and a willingness to manage risk instead of ignoring it.

If there's one idea to carry forward, it's this: a property is only a good investment when it serves a strategy. Without a plan, even a beautiful home can become a financial burden. With a plan, even a modest property can become a powerful wealth-building tool. That strategy starts with understanding why you're investing—cash flow, long-term appreciation, stability, diversification—and choosing an approach that matches your time, personality, and resources.

You've also learned that real estate isn't just "buy and collect rent." It's a full system: evaluating locations, understanding market cycles, estimating expenses honestly, preparing for vacancies, reading the fine print, and surrounding yourself with the right support—agents, lenders, inspectors, contractors, and legal or tax guidance when needed. The strongest investors aren't the ones who never face problems. They're the ones who plan for problems before they arrive, and who make decisions based on data rather than pressure or emotion.

As you move forward, keep your process simple and repeatable. Start by getting your financial foundation in order. Define your criteria. Study a market until it feels familiar. Run the numbers the same way every time. Leave room for surprises. And remember: the first deal doesn't need to be perfect—it needs to be solid, understandable, and aligned with your goals.

Most importantly, don't let "someday" become your default. Real estate is learned through action, and action starts with small, practical steps: tracking listings, talking to professionals, visiting neighborhoods, learning financing options, and building the habits that turn information into confidence.

Whether your path is active, hands-on ownership or a more passive approach, the outcome is the same: you're building assets that can outlast short-term trends and support long-term freedom. Keep learning, stay disciplined, and stay patient.

Wealth in real estate is rarely a single dramatic moment. It's the result of steady decisions—made consistently—over time. Your next step is simple: choose one action from this book and do it this week. The best investment plan is the one you actually begin.

www.ingramcontent.com/pod-product-compliance
Lightning Source LLC
LaVergne TN
LVHW022321200926
848481LV00004B/1386